KENNE
COPEL

M000082653

BREAK
/////// THE CHAIN OF
WORRY
THE JOY OF LIVING
A CAREFREE LIFE

Unless otherwise noted, all scripture is from the *King James Version* of the Bible.

Scripture quotations marked *The Amplified Bible, Classic Edition* and *AMPC* are from *The Amplified® Bible*, © 1954, 1958, 1962, 1964, 1965, 1987 by The Lockman Foundation. Used by permission.

Scripture quotations marked *New King James Version* and *NKJV* are from the *New King James Version* © 1982 by Thomas Nelson Inc.

Break the Chain of Worry
The Joy of Living a Carefree Life

ISBN 978-1-60463-330-6   30-0081
21 20 19 18 17 16   6 5 4 3 2 1

© 2016 Kenneth Copeland

Kenneth Copeland Publications
Fort Worth, TX 76192-0001

For more information about Kenneth Copeland Ministries, visit kcm.org or call 1-800-600-7395 (U.S. only) or +1-817-852-6000.

BREAK

WORRY

Outside of my wife, Gloria, I've never before dedicated a book to one specific person. But when The LORD put it on my heart to teach about breaking the worry habit, that's what He told me to do. He instructed me to begin with a tribute to one of the most worry-free, faith-filled men of God I've ever had the privilege of knowing—Bishop David Oyedepo.

Writing about him is easy, especially right now. Having recently ministered at Bishop Oyedepo's great Faith Tabernacle Church in Canaan Land, Nigeria, I'm still rejoicing over the thrill of seeing 91,000 people crowd into a

6:30 a.m. service in the middle of the pouring monsoon rains. With 54,000 in the building and 37,000 more in the overflow tents outside, it was an awesome sight—and that was just the first service. By the time everything was said and done that Sunday, 394,000 people had shown up for church.

At Faith Tabernacle those kinds of numbers aren't unusual, either. The believers there are seriously hungry to hear The WORD of God. They're so full of expectancy, God is moving among them constantly in signs, wonders and miracles—adding to the church daily as He did in the book of Acts.

What opened the door for all this to happen out in the middle of a Nigerian jungle?

One man got a revelation of his covenant with God and dared to step out on it. One man put worry behind him once and for all, and simply trusted God to do what He said He would do. Talk about a marvelous example of faith! David Oyedepo has proven The WORD will work anywhere for anyone who will believe it.

For years, he's called Gloria and me "Mom

and Dad," because right after he went into ministry he read two of our books. Somehow, he got hold of *God's Will Is Prosperity* and *The Laws of Prosperity* and The LORD used them mightily in his life. During our recent visit, he told me again how it happened.

"As a young minister I'd already come to understand The WORD of faith about healing and so forth, but I didn't yet understand the prosperity part. So I took my Bible and those two books and spent some time alone—fasting and seeking The LORD about it. As I was reading *God's Will Is Prosperity,* I realized that prosperity is a covenant. It's promised in The WORD, and since all God's promises are yes and amen through Jesus, it belongs to every believer."

For David Oyedepo, from that moment on the matter of finances was settled.

"I have a covenant with Jesus!" he explained. "It says, 'Seek first the kingdom of God and His righteousness, and all these things shall be added to you. Therefore do not worry...' (Matthew 6:33-34, *New King James Version).* Once I truly understood that, I never worried about money again."

The results have been astounding. Right in the middle of one of the most financially poor places on earth, Jesus has added enough to Bishop Oyedepo's ministry to build—debt free, by faith, and without any American money—well over $500 million worth of facilities, including not only a church but a major university. Literally hundreds of thousands of people are being taught The WORD of faith there. They're learning the laws of prosperity, putting them into action, and they're becoming what's being called "the new Nigerian middle class."

The initial 500 acres Bishop Oyedepo bought out in the bush country, which at the time was populated with nothing but a bunch of mostly unfriendly animals, has expanded to encompass more than 10,000 acres. Now called Canaan Land, it's become a city. Thriving and prospering in the midst of a natural economy that's famous for poverty, it's a testimony to the fact that God doesn't need the earth's economy to get things done. He has His own economy and it will prosper anyone who walks by faith in His WORD!

WORRY IS NO LAUGHING MATTER

"Well, Brother Copeland," someone might say, "Bishop Oyedepo is an inspiring example, but I'm just not wired like he is. I couldn't say like he did that I'm never going to worry again. My parents worried; my grandparents worried; and I've always followed in their footsteps. Sometimes I just laugh about it and say, 'What would we do without good, old worry?'"

You wouldn't be laughing if you knew what worry was doing to you. Worry is stealing from you the abundant life that belongs to you in Jesus. It's an absolutely deadly habit. It's also a sin. According to Romans 14:23, which was written to the early Church to address the question of eating meat that had been offered to idols: "He that doubteth is damned if he eat, because he eateth not of faith: for whatsoever is not of faith is sin." Or, as *The Amplified Bible, Classic Edition*, translates it, "The man who has doubts (misgivings, and uneasy conscience) about eating, and then eats...stands condemned [before God], because he is not true to his convictions and he does not act from faith. For whatever does not originate and proceed from faith is sin [whatever is done without a conviction of its approval by God is sinful]."

Think about that. Whatever does not originate from faith is sin. That means all doubt, all unbelief, and all worry is sin.

"What?! Are you saying I can't worry about anything at all?"

You can if you want to, but it's sin. Why? Because it's based on fear, and fear is of the devil. Just as faith comes from hearing and meditating on The WORD of God, fear comes from meditating on satan's lies. It walks hand in hand with unbelief and the Bible calls it *evil*.

I realize *evil* is a strong word, but I didn't come up with it. The Bible refers to it that way in the account about the 10 spies Moses sent into the Promised Land. Numbers 14:37 says the report they brought back was an "evil report." What made it evil? It was inspired by fear and not faith. Instead of assuring the Israelites the land was good and they could conquer it just like God said they would, the spies said, "Oh, the land is good all right, but it's full of giants who are too big for us to fight. We're like grasshoppers in their eyes!"

When you worry, you're essentially taking that same attitude. You're believing the devil's evil report. Rather than standing in faith on God's WORD, you're giving in to unbelief and fear.

When it comes to operating by faith or fear there is no in between. There is no neutral zone where we can just hang out and do our own thing. As human beings, we're always agreeing with either God or the devil—and the one with whom we agree is going to determine the outcome of our situation. If we agree with God and His WORD, we'll walk by faith, and whatever situation we're facing will turn out good because God is out for our total, complete, supernatural health and wealth. If we agree with the devil, we'll walk in fear and things will turn out badly because he's the thief who's come to "steal, and to kill, and to destroy" (John 10:10).

This is the reason it's impossible to please God without faith (Hebrews 11:6). It's not just because He's hardheaded about it. It's because

He loves us, and faith is what connects us with Him and enables us to receive His BLESSINGS. Fear, on the other hand, disconnects us from Him and connects us to the devil.

What we know today as fear was originally Adam's faith. A potent spiritual force, it came into manifestation on earth when Adam sinned and the forces in his spirit were perverted, or twisted opposite to the way God created them to be. (The word *wicked* actually means "twisted." That's why furniture that's made from twisted wood is referred to as *wicker.*) The first thing fear did when it came on the scene was separate Adam from God. It caused him to run and hide from God and His WORD in his time of trouble instead of running to Him for help.

If the devil had gotten his way, that would have been the end of the story. Mankind would have remained eternally separated from God and we all would have been trapped in sin and fear forever. But God loved us too much to let that happen. So He put into effect the plan He had made before the foundation of the world. He went to work to abolish fear, save us from the curse, and restore to us His BLESSING.

He made a blood covenant with Abraham and promised, "If you'll walk with Me by faith, I'll BLESS you and your seed and make you a BLESSING to all the families of the earth. I'll make you heir of the whole world" (see Genesis 12:2 and Romans 4:13). Then, as a result of what Jesus did through the cross and the resurrection, He extended that same covenant promise to all who believe on Him.

For the promise, that he should be the heir of the world, was not to Abraham, or to his seed, through the law, but through the righteousness of faith… Therefore it is of faith, that it might be by grace; to the end the promise might be sure to all the seed; not to that only which is of the law, but to that also which is of the faith of Abraham; who is the father of us all…. And if ye be Christ's, then are ye Abraham's seed, and heirs according to the promise (Romans 4:13, 16; Galatians 3:29).

A HIGH PRICE TO PAY

If you want see clearly how evil fear and worry truly are, just put yourself in God's place for a moment and consider what He did to set us free from them. Consider the price He paid to sever our connection with the devil and the curse, and to re-establish our covenant connection with Him and His BLESSING. He sacrificed His own Son. He laid the sin of all mankind upon Him and Jesus received it. He bore our sins in His own body on the tree, redeeming us from the curse: "for it is written, Cursed is every one that hangeth on a tree" (Galatians 3:13).

Jesus actually went to hell for our sakes! He went there as our substitute and suffered the pangs of death "that through death he might destroy him that had the power of death, that is, the devil; and deliver them who through fear of death were all their lifetime subject to bondage" (Hebrews 2:14-15).

When you look at it in that light, you don't have to wonder why God calls fear "evil." Wherever we allow it into our lives—whether in the area of relationships, finances or health—it makes Jesus' sacrifice of no effect in that area. It disconnects from the immeasurably precious gift of God's grace.

I once asked The LORD to define the word *grace* for me. He said, *It's My overwhelming desire to treat you as if you'd never sinned.* When we choose to worry and doubt we frustrate that desire. Even though we're born again and headed for heaven, fear will cause us to think like sinners and cut ourselves off from the heavenly BLESSINGS God intends for us to enjoy here on earth.

That's why Jesus spoke so firmly to Jairus about it. Jairus was facing a life-or-death situation. He had only one daughter, about 12 years of age, and she lay dying (Luke 8:42). Believing Jesus could heal her, Jairus asked Him to come to his house and lay His hands on her. Jesus agreed, but on the way to the house, as a crowd of people pressed in around Him, He was delayed.

A woman having an issue of blood twelve years, which had spent all her living upon physicians, neither could be healed of any, came behind him, and touched the border of his garment: and immediately her issue of blood stanched. And Jesus said, Who touched me? When all denied, Peter and they that were with him said, Master, the multitude throng thee and press thee, and sayest thou, Who touched me? And Jesus said, Somebody hath touched me: for I perceive that virtue is gone out of me. And when the woman saw that she was not hid, she came trembling, and falling down before him, she declared unto him before all the people for what cause she had touched him, and how she was healed immediately. And he said unto her, Daughter, be of good comfort: thy faith hath made thee whole; go in peace (verses 43–48).

The whole time all this was going on, Jairus was still standing there waiting…his daughter was still at lying at home getting nearer to death…and satan, who was almost certainly using the delay as an opportunity to pressure Jairus to break his faith connection with Jesus, was probably whispering worrisome thoughts into his ear: *How long is this big-mouthed woman going to talk? Is she going to tell everything that's happened the whole 12 years she's been sick? Doesn't Jesus remember your daughter's at home dying?*

Jairus, however, apparently didn't give in to the pressure. He just kept quiet. The last thing he'd said to Jesus about his daughter was, "Come and lay thy hands on her, that she may be healed; and she shall live," and he stayed with that confession. He listened to the woman's testimony about being healed of the issue of blood; he listened to what Jesus said to her; and since faith comes by hearing The WORD of God, his faith was strengthened and encouraged.

Then something happened he hadn't expected. While Jesus was speaking, a messenger came from Jairus' house, saying to him, "Thy daughter is dead; trouble not the Master" (verse 49). As a parent, I can't think of any words that would be harder to hear. For a father to get that news and still maintain control of his thinking would seem, in the natural anyway, completely impossible.

Yet that's what Jesus told Jairus to do. When He heard the little girl was dead, he answered by saying, "Fear not: believe only, and she shall be made whole" (verse 50). Sure enough, Jairus did it. He obeyed Jesus and refused to fear. As a result, a few verses later we see that his daughter was alive and well.

"Brother Copeland, I know that story is in the Bible, but I just don't understand it. How could anyone stop fear from overtaking him in a moment like that?"

The power to stop fear is in The WORD of God!

Apart from His Word, nobody can stop it. They might be able to manage it or push through it, but they won't be able to come up with the power to stop it completely. To connect with that kind of power you have to hear and put your faith in God's WORD.

That's what Jairus did. He heard the words of Jesus: "[Your daughter] shall be made whole," and he believed them. He shut fear down with faith in God, resisted the temptation to worry, and everything turned out all right.

You can see another example of this in the life of Peter.

Remember when he walked on the water? Just before he did that he was scared out of his wits. So were the other disciples who were with him in the boat. They not only had a stormy sea to deal with, as Matthew 14 tells it:

> *In the fourth watch of the night Jesus went unto them, walking on the sea. And when the disciples saw him walking on the sea, they were troubled, saying, It is a spirit; and they cried out for fear. But straightway Jesus spake unto them, saying, Be of good cheer; it is I; be not afraid. And Peter answered him and said, LORD, if it be thou, bid me come unto thee on the water. And he said, Come. And when Peter was come down out of the ship, he walked on the water, to go to Jesus (verses 25-29).*

In that instance, the power of God's WORD not only destroyed Peter's fear, it carried him across water. Right out there in the middle of the Sea of Galilee He walked on the word *come*, and never even got his feet wet. But then, he let his natural, carnal mind take over. He got his attention off The WORD, started worrying about the waves, and began to sink. He got into fear, it separated him from the power he was walking on, and he was immediately in trouble.

FEAR TOLERATED IS FAITH CONTAMINATED

A number of years ago, right after the 9/11 attacks in New York City, God dealt with me about stripping fear from the Body of Christ. He made it part of my mandate and said to me in a way that still reverberates inside me, *Fear tolerated is faith contaminated!* As Peter learned out there on the Sea of Galilee, when fear is mixed with faith, faith stops working. Fear weakens it and contaminates it so that it can't get the job done.

That's the reason worry is such a bad habit. When you worry, you're ministering fear to yourself. You're thinking about bad things and picturing them coming to pass in your life. You're envisioning yourself losing your job, for instance, and running short of money. You're talking about it and making fear confessions: "I'm just worried to death about all these dumb decisions the government's making. They're messing up the economy so badly I'm afraid my company is going to go under and I'm going to end up unemployed."

No matter what the government is doing, you, as a believer, don't have any business saying such things! It's counterproductive. It doesn't proceed from faith and, as we've already seen, whatever doesn't proceed from faith is sin.

"But getting rid of worry altogether just isn't realistic!" someone might say. "It can't be done."

Yes, it can. Jairus proved it. If he could refuse to worry in the midst of what he was facing, anyone can do it, anytime—including you and me.

"Jairus had an advantage, though, Brother Copeland. He was in the presence of Jesus."

Sure he was. But I know people who, because they're born again and filled with the Holy Spirit, have Jesus with them all the time and they've practically made worrying a career. So it's not just Jesus' presence that makes the difference. It's His WORD, and when it comes to worrying, He's said the same thing to every believer He said to Jairus.

"Fear not, only believe!"

The fact that He commanded it means we can do it. If He commanded us to do something and left us without the ability to obey, it would be unjust. Therefore, anything He tells us to do He empowers us to do by giving us His WORD.

Look through the Bible and you'll see this is

God's pattern: He always gives His WORD first, to bring faith, before He gives a command. Think again about how He dealt with David Oyedepo and you'll see what I mean. The first thing God did for him where prosperity was concerned was speak to him through the words of Jesus in Matthew 6:33: "Seek ye first the kingdom of God, and His righteousness, and all these things shall be added unto you."

Bishop Oyedepo received those words as a covenant promise, and they caused faith to arise in his heart. They empowered him to believe that everything he needed would be added to him. As a result, he was able to obey the command in verse 34, "Do not worry" *(NKJV);* and never worry about finances again.

"But you don't understand," someone might say, "they're going to repossess my car!"

What does that have to do with anything?

"Well, I need a car to get to work."

Don't you think Jesus knows that?

"Yeah…but…"

There's the problem, right there! It's not your need of a car. It's your compromising, "yeah, but" attitude toward God's WORD and His covenant promise of provision.

Back in 1967, when I was a student at Oral Roberts University, I heard Brother Roberts say something about compromise I'll never forget. He was preaching about the three young Hebrew men who were thrown into the fiery furnace for refusing to bow to the king's idol, and how Jesus, as "the fourth man," showed up to deliver them. Right in the middle of his sermon he said this: "Whatever you compromise to keep, you will eventually lose!"

Suddenly, on the inside of me, I saw these words like they were on a signpost: *The Uncompromised WORD of God.* "LORD, what does that mean?" I asked. "How could I compromise Your WORD?"

You compromise it when you choose not to believe it, He answered. *When you see My WORD says that by My stripes you were healed and you say, "Yeah, but, God I'm sick," you compromise that WORD. You put more faith in the symptoms in your body than in what I said. As a result, you lose out on the healing I've provided for you.*

Recently, I was ministering about this on our daily television broadcast and The LORD spoke to me about it again. He said through a word of prophecy:

Don't compromise My WORD. Take it. Choose to believe it, and that WORD will change the facts and bring itself to pass in your life. Agree with Me and I'll take your word and My WORD, put them together, and faith will come and separate you from the enemy, from the devil who is the spirit of darkness, sickness and lack. He's the one who is causing you trouble and he's connected to the sin of fear. So reject all fear, begin to change what you say, and I'll change what's happening to you. I'll change your circumstances if you will listen to Me.

THE DEVIL'S ONLY STRATEGY

The devil can't do anything to you apart from fear any more than God can do something for you apart from faith. That's why he works so desperately to steal The WORD from you. He knows that because faith comes from hearing The WORD, if he can separate you from The WORD he can disconnect you from God's power and BLESSING. He can get you trapped in worry and unbelief where God can't do much for you.

To see what that looks like, read about the people who lived in Nazareth during Jesus' ministry. They had the Master Himself right there in their synagogue, preaching under the greatest Anointing the earth had ever seen, but "He could there do no mighty work [among them] because of their unbelief" (Mark 6:5-6). Notice that verse doesn't say Jesus *wouldn't* do any mighty works in Nazareth. It says He *couldn't*. Why? Because they didn't believe what He said. Like the Israelites who didn't go into the Promised Land because they feared the giants, they let the devil steal The WORD and faith from them and "limited the Holy One of Israel" (Psalm 78:41).

According to Mark 4, this is satan's only strategy. Whenever the seed of God's WORD is sown in people's hearts, he comes after it immediately to get it away from them. He tries either to steal it or to convince the hearers to compromise The WORD in some way so that it doesn't bear fruit. One of the ways he does it is with worry. He uses "the cares and anxieties of the world and distractions of the age…[to] choke and suffocate The WORD, and it becomes fruitless" (verse 19, *AMPC*).

The Greek word translated *cares and anxieties* is literally defined as "an over-engrossing mental affair." That definition accurately describes what worry does. When you give place to it, it engrosses your mind. It takes over your thinking the way weeds take over a garden. You may not even notice at the time what's happening. You're still going to church on Sunday and reading your Bible every morning, so you're still hearing The WORD. Everything appears to be fine. Yet something has changed. The WORD isn't producing faith in you like it used to. You've been choking it out by rehearsing all the worries that the devil has been feeding you.

To make matters worse, by meditating on the devil's lies you've given him access to your innermost counsel. You've tuned in to his voice instead of tuning in to The WORD and the voice of the Holy Spirit. You've given satan access to your thoughts rather than God.

As a result, every time you turn around you find you're thinking of new problems to worry about. As satan keeps grinding away at you about them, the fear level increases, undermines your faith, and—here's the irony of it—separates you further from the only power that can solve those problems.

It's a cruel and dangerous cycle. But praise God, the Bible tells us how to break out of it. It says:

> ...Be clothed with humility: for God resisteth the proud, and giveth grace to the humble. Humble yourselves therefore under the mighty hand of God, that he may exalt you in due time: Casting all your care upon him; for he careth for you. Be sober, be vigilant; because your adversary the devil, as a roaring lion, walketh about, seeking whom he may devour:

Whom resist stedfast in the faith, knowing that the same afflictions are accomplished in your brethren that are in the world. But the God of all grace, who hath called us unto his eternal glory by Christ Jesus, after that ye have suffered a while, make you perfect, stablish, strengthen, settle you. To him be glory and dominion for ever and ever. Amen (1 Peter 5:5-11).

Notice, the first thing that passage tells us to do is humble ourselves. Why do we have to humble ourselves to get free of worry? Because in God's eyes, continuing to worry and carry care is pride! Worrying is ignoring The WORD. Worry ignores the fact that God laid every care, sin, sickness, money problem and anything else that's under the curse on Jesus, and tries to carry those things and fix them with natural human strength.

Whatever you're worrying about, if you had the ability you would have already fixed it. So stop running around in mental circles fretting about it, and just humble yourself before God. Acknowledge that without Him you don't have the spiritual power to overcome the things that are troubling you. Then cast on Him "the whole of your care [all your anxieties, all your worries, all your concerns, once and for all]" (verse 7, *AMPC*).

Don't just give Him half of your care and try to carry the rest yourself. Don't give them to Him one minute and then take them back the next. That's not what the Scripture says. It says we're to cast the whole of our care on Him "once and for all."

That means we should never have a care. *Ever!*

I'M NOT CARRYING ANY LOAD

In addition to Bishop Oyedepo, one of the best examples I've seen of this kind of carefree living was Brother Kenneth E. Hagin. As a young boy lying paralyzed on his bed with a deformed heart and dying of an incurable blood disease, he got a revelation of the fact that worry was a sin. God revealed it to him while he was searching The WORD hoping to find out how to get healed.

At the time, he didn't yet know anything

about faith because he'd never heard anyone preach it. The only thing he'd ever heard from the ministers who'd come to visit him was that he was going to die, and he worried about it every day. In his mind's eye, he'd imagine his family finding him dead and taking his body to the funeral home. He'd see his funeral and see himself lying in the casket. He'd envision the gravesite with everyone crying as the casket was being lowered into the ground.

Eventually, because he kept reading and meditating on The WORD, he woke up to what he was doing. He realized that by worrying he was disobeying God's command. Determined not to give place to that sin anymore, he prayed and said, "God, if You'll forgive me for this worry fit and pity party, if You'll forgive me for crying all day long about my sorry lot in life, I commit to You I will never worry again as long as I live on this earth."

That was in 1933, and from then on he testified, "I haven't worried a day since!"

Not long after he gave up worrying at 16 years old, he saw in Mark 11:24 that he could believe for healing and receive it, so he did. Then he went out preaching The WORD of faith. Later in his life, after he started Rhema Bible School, he told about a time when some ministers came to tour the campus. As he was showing them around, they were looking at all the construction that was going on. Thinking about the cost involved, one of them said, "Brother Hagin, I just can't imagine the load you're carrying with this ministry."

"I'm not carrying any load!" he laughed. "I turned all this over to Jesus. This Bible School was His idea, not mine. I figure if He can't make it go it will just have to flop because I'm not taking the care."

It's no wonder Brother Hagin enjoyed such outstanding success in his life and ministry! He obeyed 1 Peter 5:5-11. He humbled himself under God's mighty hand and cast all his cares once and for all on God. So, God did for him just what He said He'd do. He exalted him over all the cares of this world. He lifted him up over the curse and into THE BLESSING.

"Well, that's wonderful," you might say, "but my faith just isn't as strong as Brother Hagin's was."

Then get into God's WORD. Just as meditating on the lies of the devil will weaken your faith, meditating on The WORD will make it stronger. Remember, the power to break the worry habit is in The WORD! It carries within it the power to bring itself to pass, so get it on the inside of you in abundance.

Find scriptures that cover the cares that you've been carrying. Make a list of them. Keep them in front of your eyes and in your mouth until they're rooted in your heart. The WORD is the "sword of the spirit" (Ephesians 6:17). If you grab hold of it and hang on to it, The WORD will fight its own fight.

If you want to see what The WORD can do for you, read the story of Joshua. When it came time for him to lead the Israelites into the Promised Land, the sword of The WORD was the first thing The LORD talked to him about. Reminding him that He'd already sworn in His covenant to give the Israelites that land, He said:

Every place that the sole of your foot shall tread upon, that have I given unto you, as I said unto

Moses.... There shall not any man be able to stand before thee all the days of thy life: as I was with Moses, so I will be with thee: I will not fail thee, nor forsake thee. Be strong and of a good courage: for unto this people shalt thou divide for an inheritance the land, which I sware unto their fathers to give them. Only be thou strong and very courageous, that thou mayest observe to do according to all the law, which Moses my servant commanded thee: turn not from it to the right hand or to the left, that thou mayest prosper whithersoever thou goest. This book of the law shall not depart out of thy mouth; but thou shalt meditate therein day and night, that thou mayest observe to do according to all that is written therein: for then thou shalt make thy way prosperous, and then thou shalt have good success (Joshua 1:3, 5-8).

Joshua was just as human as you and I are, so I'm sure he had some natural considerations about going into the Promised Land. After all, the last time he was there—40 years earlier when he, Caleb and the other 10 spies had gone to spy it out—he'd seen giants there. He'd seen walled cities and strong enemies. So, from a human perspective, Joshua probably had some questions. He might have been wondering, *Have those giants gotten bigger over the past 40 years? Have the cities gotten stronger? What's going on there?*

Rather than addressing those questions, however, God directed Joshua to His WORD. He got Joshua's mind off the potential problems and onto His Promise. He commanded him to not let that Promise out of his sight, but to keep it in his mouth day and night and then he would have good success. He would, as *The Amplified Bible, Classic Edition* puts it, "deal wisely and have good success."

THE WORD
ALWAYS WORKS

If you keep The WORD on your mind like Joshua did, it will do the same for you. It will enable you to deal wisely in all the affairs of life. It will also cause your faith to go out before you so that God can prepare the way for you.

Look a little further at what God did for the Israelites when He told them to take the Promised Land and you'll see what I mean. They found out after wandering around 40 years in the wilderness worrying about giants, that the whole time the giants had been afraid of them. The two men of faith that Joshua sent ahead to scope out the situation in Jericho met a woman there who confirmed it. "I know that The LORD hath given you the land," she said.

> *Your terror is fallen upon us, and that all the inhabitants of the land faint because of you. For we have heard how The LORD dried up the water of the Red sea for you, when ye came out of Egypt; and what ye did unto the two kings of the Amorites, that were on the other side Jordan, Sihon and Og, whom ye utterly destroyed. And as soon as we had heard these things, our hearts did melt, neither did there remain any more courage in any man, because of you: for The LORD your God, he is God in heaven above, and in earth beneath (Joshua 2:9-11).*

Remember this: Once God has given the command and you're obeying it in faith, God isn't just working *on* you, He's working *for* you. He's out ahead of you, paving the way for your victory. That's something people with worried, fear-ridden minds don't think about. Like the first 10 unbelieving spies Moses sent into the Promised Land, all they're thinking is *We're like grasshoppers!* All they're seeing is the giants.

The Israelites could have gone into the Promised Land 40 years earlier, and the giants of Jericho would have bowed down and surrendered to them. They would have said to the Israelites, "All we have is yours." But it didn't happen because that first bunch of Israelites had grasshoppers on their mind. They were worrying about the problems instead of meditating on God's Promise. They were considering what they saw and felt instead of The WORD.

You and I don't have to make the same mistake. Instead of wandering around for years in a wilderness of worry we can break the worry habit now. We can take our stand on the blood covenant Promises in The WORD of God, cast all our cares once and for all on Him, and covenant with Him never to worry again.

How do you take the first step?

Take Communion over it. But don't do it quickly or lightly. Before you go before The LORD with Communion elements, spend some serious time reading these scriptures and meditating on them. Ask the Holy Spirit to help you identify every care or worry you've been carrying. As He brings them to your mind, write them down, and prepare yourself to hand them over to The LORD. Include everything—from big issues like the national economy, your health, and what's happening in your family, to problems as minor as what to do about your unruly hair. Next to every item you write down, make note of the Scriptural promises that cover it.

When you sense you're ready, take that list to The LORD. Get on your knees before Him with the Communion elements and make a quality commitment by praying something like this:

Heavenly Father, I take You at Your WORD and at Your command. I thank You that the body of Jesus was broken for me, that He took the curse for me and shed His blood to pay the price for me, and because of what He's done I never have to worry again. I thank You that You've given me Your WORD that if I cast my cares over on You and resist the devil's pressure to pick them back up again, You will exalt me over every care and every adverse situation. In this blood and by the power of this WORD, in the Name of The LORD Jesus Christ, with the help of the Greater One who lives within me and the abundant supply of Your grace, I will never worry, be concerned, or anxious about anything again.

Father, I boldly declare this by faith. From this moment on I trust You, Sir, to interrupt, stop, or correct me in any way necessary, to get my attention should I ever begin to worry about anything. As You do, I commit to You that I will deal with it immediately. I will not let the sun go down with worry on my mind. In Jesus' Name. Amen.

Once you've prayed, start walking out your commitment by obeying the command in Philippians 4:6-8:

> *Do not fret or have any anxiety about anything, but in every circumstance and in*

everything, by prayer and petition (definite requests), with thanksgiving, continue to make your wants known to God. And God's peace [shall be yours, that tranquil state of a soul assured of its salvation through Christ, and so fearing nothing from God and being content with its earthly lot of whatever sort that is, that peace] which transcends all understanding shall garrison and mount guard over your hearts and minds in Christ Jesus. For the rest, brethren, whatever is true, whatever is worthy of reverence and is honorable and seemly, whatever is just, whatever is pure, whatever is lovely and lovable, whatever is kind and winsome and gracious, if there is any virtue and excellence, if there is anything worthy of praise, think on and weigh and take account of these things [fix your minds on them] (AMPC).

This is the process of living a carefree life. This is how you wipe out worry completely. You rejoice always—it's impossible to rejoice and worry at the same time—and then you guard your thoughts. If a worry starts to arise, you say, "No, that's not a good report. I'm not going to think on it. I take authority over it and I'm not going to touch it with my mind anymore."

Is that kind of vigilance really possible?

It wouldn't be if you were trying to do it in the flesh, in your own natural strength, but you aren't. You're doing it in the spirit. You're doing it by the power of God's WORD with the help of the Holy Ghost. As 2 Corinthians 10:4-5 says, "(For the weapons of our warfare are not carnal, but mighty through God to the pulling down of strong holds;) Casting down imaginations, and every high thing that exalteth itself against the knowledge of God, and bringing into captivity every thought to the obedience of Christ."

Granted, at times the warfare involved in taking your thoughts captive can be intense. But you can win every battle if, instead of just fighting thoughts with thoughts, you open your mouth and fight them with God's spoken WORD. When you speak Scripture it brings authority on the scene. God listens. The angels listen. And, like it or not, the devil has to listen, too.

The book of Psalms says, "Out of the mouth of babes and sucklings hast thou ordained strength [or praise] because of thine enemies, that thou mightest still the enemy and the avenger....I will be glad and rejoice in thee: I will sing praise to thy name, O thou most High. When mine enemies are turned back, they shall fall and perish at thy presence" (Psalm 8:2, 9:2-3).

The devil flees when you quote The WORD! It's too strong for him. He can't stand up against it. So when he hounds you with worrisome thoughts, give him an earful of it. I don't care if it's the middle of the night, praise God out loud! Declare The WORD, and before long the devil will pack up his stuff and get out. Once he's gone, just leave everything with Jesus. Say, "LORD, I turn this over to You and trust You to fix it. Good night!"

"Brother Copeland, isn't that a little irresponsible?"

No! It's the most responsible thing you can do. I learned that early in my faith life when our son, John, was a little boy and he came down with scarlet fever. His skin turned as red as a strawberry and felt like crepe paper. He hurt so bad that any kind of light shining on him caused him pain. I'd pray over him and he'd get a little better, but then he'd get worse again.

One night, I was up praying over him off and on for most of the night. I'd lay hands on him and believe God for his healing, go back to bed, and get up again a little while later to check on him because I was worried. Finally, The LORD said, *You rolled the care of his healing over on Me. Why didn't you leave it with Me? Every time you go in and check on him, you're taking it out of My hands.*

I saw what He was saying and made the change. I went in one more time, laid hands on John and said, "In the Name of The LORD Jesus Christ of Nazareth, this boy is healed, and I thank You for it, LORD. You're my healer and You're his healer, so I roll all the care of this on You."

An hour later, I woke up and started to jump up and go check on him again. But this time I caught myself. I laid back down in the bed and said, "No! Jesus, this is Your care. I've given it to You and I trust You with it."

Of course, the next split second the devil spoke up. "You're a sorry parent!" he said. "What if that boy's cover has fallen off and he's cold?"

"It's not my care!" I answered. "Let the angels put the cover back on him. I'm trusting Jesus to take care of this."

The next morning I went to preach the morning service, and after it was over I felt a tug on my coat. I turned around and it was John. "Look at me, Daddy!" he said, pulling up his shirt to show me his skin. "Look at me, Daddy! I'm healed!"

That's the kind of thing that happens when you stop worrying and roll the care over on Jesus. So stick with the process. Take every imagination, thought, dream, idea or anything else contrary to what you're believing for in your life and cast it down. Even if you have to do it every 30 seconds for a while—DO IT! You'll be shocked at how quickly, as your faith rises and takes command, you can crush the worry habit and live a supernaturally carefree life!

Prayer for Salvation and Baptism in the Holy Spirit

Heavenly Father, I come to You in the Name of Jesus. Your Word says, "Whosoever shall call on the name of the Lord shall be saved" (Acts 2:21). I am calling on You. I pray and ask Jesus to come into my heart and be Lord over my life according to Romans 10:9-10: "If thou shalt confess with thy mouth the Lord Jesus, and shalt believe in thine heart that God hath raised him from the dead, thou shalt be saved. For with the heart man believeth unto righteousness; and with the mouth confession is made unto salvation." I do that now. I confess that Jesus is Lord, and I believe in my heart that God raised Him from the dead. I repent of sin. I renounce it. I renounce the devil and everything he stands for. Jesus is my Lord.

I am now reborn! I am a Christian—a child of Almighty God! I am saved! You also said in Your Word, "If ye then, being evil, know how to give good gifts unto your children: HOW MUCH MORE shall your heavenly Father give the Holy Spirit to them that ask him?" (Luke 11:13). I'm also asking You to fill me with the Holy Spirit. Holy Spirit, rise up within me as I praise God. I fully expect to speak with other tongues as You give me the utterance (Acts 2:4). In Jesus' Name. Amen!

Begin to praise God for filling you with the Holy Spirit. Speak those words and syllables you receive—not in your own language, but the language given to you by the Holy Spirit. You have to use your own voice. God will not force you to speak. Don't be concerned with how it sounds. It is a heavenly language!

Continue with the blessing God has given you and pray in the spirit every day.

You are a born-again, Spirit-filled believer. You'll never be the same!

Find a good church that boldly preaches God's Word and obeys it. Become part of a church family who will love and care for you as you love and care for them.

We need to be connected to each other. It increases our strength in God. It's God's plan for us.

Make it a habit to watch the Believer's Voice of Victory Network television broadcast and become a doer of the Word, who is blessed in his doing (James 1:22-25).

About the Author

Kenneth Copeland is co-founder and president of Kenneth Copeland Ministries in Fort Worth, Texas, and best-selling author of books that include *Honor— Walking in Honesty, Truth and Integrity,* and *THE BLESSING of The LORD Makes Rich and He Adds No Sorrow With It.*

Since 1967, Kenneth has been a minister of the gospel of Christ and teacher of God's WORD. He is also the artist on award-winning albums such as his Grammy-nominated *Only the Redeemed, In His Presence, He Is Jehovah, Just a Closer Walk* and *Big Band Gospel.* He also co-stars as the character Wichita Slim in the children's adventure videos *The Gunslinger, Covenant Rider* and the movie *The Treasure of Eagle Mountain,* and as Daniel Lyon in the Commander Kellie and the Superkids_{TM} videos *Armor of Light* and *Judgment: The Trial of Commander Kellie.* Kenneth also co-stars as a Hispanic godfather in the 2009 and 2016 movies *The Rally* and *The Rally 2: Breaking the Curse.*

With the help of offices and staff in the United States, Canada, England, Australia, South Africa, Ukraine, Singapore and Latin America Kenneth is fulfilling his vision to boldly preach the uncompromised WORD of God from the top of this world, to the bottom, and all the way around. His ministry reaches millions of people worldwide through daily and Sunday TV broadcasts, magazines, teaching audios and videos, conventions and campaigns, and the World Wide Web.

Learn more about Kenneth Copeland Ministries by visiting our website at **kcm.org.**

When the Lord first spoke to Kenneth and Gloria Copeland about starting the *Believer's Voice of Victory* magazine...

He said: *This is your seed. Give it to everyone who ever responds to your ministry, and don't ever allow anyone to pay for a subscription!*

For more than 45 years, it has been the joy of Kenneth Copeland Ministries to bring the good news to believers. Readers enjoy teaching from ministers who write from lives of living contact with God, and testimonies from believers experiencing victory through God's Word in their everyday lives.

Today, the *BVOV* magazine is mailed monthly, bringing encouragement and blessing to believers around the world. Many even use it as a ministry tool, passing it on to others who desire to know Jesus and grow in their faith!

Request your FREE subscription to the *Believer's Voice of Victory* magazine today!

Go to **freevictory.com** to subscribe online, or call us at **1-800-600-7395** (U.S. only) or **+1-817-852-6000**.

We're Here for You!®

Your growth in God's Word and your victory in Jesus are at the very center of our hearts. In every way God has equipped us, we will help you deal with the issues facing you, so you can be the **victorious overcomer** He has planned for you to be.

The mission of Kenneth Copeland Ministries is about all of us growing and going together. Our prayer is that you will take full advantage of all The LORD has given us to share with you.

Wherever you are in the world, you can watch the *Believer's Voice of Victory* broadcast on television (check your local listings), the Internet at kcm.org or on our digital Roku channel.

Our website, **kcm.org,** gives you access to every resource we've developed for your victory. And, you can find contact information for our international offices in Africa, Asia, Australia, Canada, Europe, Latin America, Ukraine and our headquarters in the United States.

Each office is staffed with devoted men and women, ready to serve and pray with you. You can contact the worldwide office nearest you for assistance, and you can call us for prayer at our U.S. number +1-817-852-6000, 24 hours every day!

We encourage you to connect with us often and let us be part of your everyday walk of faith!

Jesus Is LORD!

Kenneth & Gloria Copeland

Kenneth and Gloria Copeland